CH00430815

|  |  |  |  |
|--|--|--|--|
| .................................... | .................................... | .................................... |  |
| .................................... | .................................... | .................................... |  |
| .................................... | .................................... | .................................... |  |
| .................................... | .................................... | .................................... |  |
| .................................... | .................................... | .................................... |  |
| .................................... | .................................... | .................................... |  |
| .................................... | .................................... | .................................... |  |
| .................................... | .................................... | .................................... |  |
| .................................... | .................................... | .................................... |  |
| .................................... | .................................... | .................................... |  |
| .................................... | .................................... | .................................... |  |
| .................................... | .................................... | .................................... |  |
| .................................... | .................................... | .................................... |  |
| .................................... | .................................... | .................................... |  |
| .................................... | .................................... | .................................... |  |
| .................................... | .................................... | .................................... |  |
| .................................... | .................................... | .................................... |  |
| .................................... | .................................... | .................................... |  |

**Nottinghamshire County Council**

DP&P(O) 03.10/Comms/4261

# County Library

Please return / renew by the
last date shown.

# Balm for the

# Troubled Soul

Verses from the Scriptures

*Compiled by N.I. Nwokolo*

Matador
5 Weir Road
Kibworth Beauchamp
Leicester LE8 0LQ, UK
Tel: (+44) 116 279 2299
Fax: (+44) 116 279 2277
Email: books@troubador.co.uk
Web: www.troubador.co.uk/matador

ISBN 978 1848766 891

British Library Cataloguing in Publication Data.
A catalogue record for this book is available from the British Library.

Typeset in 10pt StempelGaramond Roman by Troubador Publishing Ltd, Leicester, UK

**Matador** is an imprint of Troubador Publishing Ltd

Printed in Great Britain by the MPG Books Group, Bodmin and King's Lynn

# Contents

# Comfort

Come unto me, all ye that labour and are heavy laden, and I will give you rest.
*Matthew 11:28*

Peace I leave with you, my peace I give unto you: not as the world giveth, give I unto you. Let not your heart be troubled, neither let it be afraid.
*John 14:27*

God is our refuge and strength, a very present help in trouble.
*Psalm 46:1*

I will lift up mine eyes unto the hills, from whence cometh my help. My help cometh from the LORD, which made heaven and earth.
*Psalm 121:1-2*

He healeth the broken in heart, and bindeth up their wounds.
*Psalm 147:3*

Fear thou not; for I am with thee: be not dismayed; for I am thy God: I will strengthen thee; yea, I will help thee; yea, I will uphold thee with the right hand of my righteousness.
*Isaiah 41:10*

Yea, I have loved thee with an everlasting love: therefore with lovingkindness have I drawn thee.
*Jeremiah 31:3*

Can a woman forget her sucking child, that she should not have compassion on the son of her womb? yea, they may forget, yet will I not forget thee.
*Isaiah 49:15*

Behold, I have graven thee upon the palms of my hands; thy walls are continually before me.
*Isaiah 49:16*

The eternal God is thy refuge, and underneath are the everlasting arms:
*Deuteronomy 33:27*

Whereas thou hast been forsaken and hated, so that no man went through thee, I will make thee an eternal excellency, a joy of many generations.
*Isaiah 60:15*


Be still, and know that I am God:
*Psalm 46:10*


As one whom his mother comforteth, so will I comfort you;
*Isaiah 66:13*


For he satisfieth the longing soul, and filleth the hungry soul with goodness.
*Psalm 107:9*


Like as a father pitieth his children, so the LORD pitieth them that fear him.
*Psalm 103:13*


A father of the fatherless, and a judge of the widows, is God in his holy habitation.
*Psalm 68:5*

For the LORD hath called thee as a woman forsaken and grieved in spirit, and a wife of youth, when thou wast refused, saith thy God.
*Isaiah 54:6*

Behold, what manner of love the Father hath bestowed upon us, that we should be called the sons of God:
*1 John 3:1*

The Spirit of the Lord GOD is upon me; because the LORD hath anointed me to preach good tidings unto the meek; he hath sent me to bind up the brokenhearted, to proclaim liberty to the captives, and the opening of the prison to them that are bound;
*Isaiah 61:1*

Which of you by taking thought can add one cubit unto his stature?
*Matthew 6:27*

Let not your heart be troubled: ye believe in God, believe also in me.
*John 14:1*

For the Father himself loveth you, because ye have loved me, and have believed that I came out from God.
*John 16:27*


The LORD upholdeth all that fall, and raiseth up all those that be bowed down.
*Psalm 145:14*


They that trust in the LORD shall be as mount Zion, which cannot be removed, but abideth for ever.
*Psalm 125:1*


Thou wilt keep him in perfect peace, whose mind is stayed on thee: because he trusteth in thee.
*Isaiah 26:3*


And they that know thy name will put their trust in thee: for thou, LORD, hast not forsaken them that seek thee.
*Psalm 9:10*

The LORD is my shepherd; I shall not want.
He maketh me to lie down in green pastures:
he leadeth me beside the still waters.
He restoreth my soul: he leadeth me in the paths of
righteousness for his name's sake.
*Psalm 23:1-3*

Blessed are they that mourn: for they shall be comforted.
*Matthew 5:4*

Blessed be God, even the Father of our Lord Jesus
Christ, the Father of mercies, and the God of all
comfort;
Who comforteth us in all our tribulation, that we
may be able to comfort them which are in any
trouble, by the comfort wherewith we ourselves are
comforted of God.
*2 Corinthians 1:3-4*

For God hath not given us the spirit of fear; but of
power, and of love, and of a sound mind.
*2 Timothy 1:7*

Thou art my father, my God, and the rock of my
salvation.
*Psalm 89:26*

Trust in the LORD with all thine heart; and lean not unto thine own understanding. In all thy ways acknowledge him, and he shall direct thy paths.
*Proverbs 3:5-6*


Behold, God is my salvation; I will trust, and not be afraid:
*Isaiah 12:2*


Thou shalt increase my greatness, and comfort me on every side.
*Psalm 71:21*


I will never leave thee, nor forsake thee.
*Hebrews 13:5*


And I will pray the Father, and he shall give you another Comforter, that he may abide with you for ever;
*John 14:16*


I will not leave you comfortless: I will come to you.
*John 14:18*

And, lo, I am with you always, even unto the end of the world. Amen.
*Matthew 28:20*

# Hope

Why art thou cast down, O my soul? and why art
thou disquieted within me? hope thou in God: for I
shall yet praise him, who is the health of my
countenance, and my God.
*Psalm 42:11*

Be of good courage, and he shall strengthen your
heart, all ye that hope in the LORD.
*Psalm 31:24*

For I the LORD thy God will hold thy right hand,
saying unto thee, Fear not; I will help thee.
*Isaiah 41:13*

For I know the thoughts that I think toward you,
saith the LORD, thoughts of peace, and not of evil,
to give you an expected end.
*Jeremiah 29:11*

The LORD will perfect that which concerneth me:
*Psalm 138:8*

He hath made every thing beautiful in his time:
*Ecclesiastes 3:11*


For his anger endureth but a moment; in his favour
is life: weeping may endure for a night, but joy
cometh in the morning.
*Psalm 30:5*


I will instruct thee and teach thee in the way which
thou shalt go: I will guide thee with mine eye.
*Psalm 32:8*


Cast thy burden upon the LORD, and he shall
sustain thee: he shall never suffer the righteous to
be moved.
*Psalm 55:22*


The LORD will give strength unto his people;
the LORD will bless his people with peace.
*Psalm 29:11*

Be strong and of a good courage; be not afraid,
neither be thou dismayed: for the LORD thy God
is with thee whithersoever thou goest.
*Joshua 1:9*


Commit thy way unto the LORD; trust also in
him; and he shall bring it to pass.
*Psalm 37:5*


I can do all things through Christ which
strengtheneth me.
*Philippians 4:13*


Trust in the LORD with all thine heart; and lean
not unto thine own understanding.  In all thy ways
acknowledge him, and he shall direct thy paths.
*Proverbs 3:5-6*


But they that wait upon the LORD shall renew
their strength; they shall mount up with wings as
eagles; they shall run, and not be weary; and they
shall walk, and not faint.
*Isaiah 40:31*

Remember ye not the former things, neither consider the things of old. Behold, I will do a new thing; now it shall spring forth; shall ye not know it? I will even make a way in the wilderness, and rivers in the desert.
*Isaiah 43:18-19*

For the mountains shall depart, and the hills be removed; but my kindness shall not depart from thee, neither shall the covenant of my peace be removed, saith the LORD that hath mercy on thee.
*Isaiah 54:10*

Take therefore no thought for the morrow: for the morrow shall take thought for the things of itself. Sufficient unto the day is the evil thereof.
*Matthew 6:34*

Thy word is a lamp unto my feet, and a light unto my path.
*Psalm 119:105*

For whatsoever things were written aforetime were written for our learning, that we through patience and comfort of the scriptures might have hope.
*Romans 15:4*

God is not a man, that he should lie; neither the son of man, that he should repent: hath he said, and shall he not do it? or hath he spoken, and shall he not make it good?
*Numbers 23:19*


Blessed is every one that feareth the LORD; that walketh in his ways.  For thou shalt eat the labour of thine hands: happy shalt thou be, and it shall be well with thee.
*Psalm 128:1-2*


The fear of the LORD is the beginning of wisdom:
*Proverbs 9:10*


For by me thy days shall be multiplied, and the years of thy life shall be increased.
*Proverbs 9:11*


Humble yourselves therefore under the mighty hand of God, that he may exalt you in due time: Casting all your care upon him; for he careth for you.
*1 Peter 5:7*

Thou hast turned for me my mourning into dancing: thou hast put off my sackcloth, and girded me with gladness;
*Psalm 30:11*


For this God is our God for ever and ever: he will be our guide even unto death.
*Psalm 48:14*


Thou shalt guide me with thy counsel, and afterward receive me to glory.
*Psalm 73:24*


Surely goodness and mercy shall follow me all the days of my life: and I will dwell in the house of the LORD for ever.
*Psalm 23:6*

# Healing

Is any thing too hard for the LORD?
*Genesis 18:14*

And ye shall serve the LORD your God, and he
shall bless thy bread, and thy water; and I will take
sickness away from the midst of thee.
*Exodus 23:25*

I am the LORD that healeth thee.
*Exodus 15:26*

Bless the LORD, O my soul, and forget not all his
benefits:
Who forgiveth all thine iniquities; who healeth all
thy diseases;
*Psalm 103:2-3*

O LORD my God, I cried unto thee, and thou hast
healed me.
*Psalm 30:2*

My son, attend to my words; incline thine ear unto my sayings.

Let them not depart from thine eyes; keep them in the midst of thine heart.

For they are life unto those that find them, and health to all their flesh.

*Proverbs 4:20-22*


Surely he hath borne our griefs, and carried our sorrows: yet we did esteem him stricken, smitten of God, and afflicted.

But he was wounded for our transgressions, he was bruised for our iniquities: the chastisement of our peace was upon him; and with his stripes we are healed.

*Isaiah 53:4-5*


That it might be fulfilled which was spoken by Esaias the prophet, saying, Himself took our infirmities, and bare our sicknesses.

*Matthew 8:17*


For he hath not despised nor abhorred the affliction of the afflicted; neither hath he hid his face from him; but when he cried unto him, he heard.

*Psalm 22:24*

This is my comfort in my affliction: for thy word hath quickened me.
*Psalm 119:50*

Unless thy law had been my delights, I should then have perished in mine affliction.
*Psalm 119:92*

The fear of the LORD prolongeth days:
*Proverbs 10:27*

I shall not die, but live, and declare the works of the LORD.
*Psalm 118:17*

For I will restore health unto thee, and I will heal thee of thy wounds, saith the LORD; because they called thee an Outcast, saying, This is Zion, whom no man seeketh after.
*Jeremiah 30:17*

But unto you that fear my name shall the Sun of righteousness arise with healing in his wings; and ye shall go forth, and grow up as calves of the stall.
*Malachi 4:2*

When the even was come, they brought unto him many that were possessed with devils: and he cast out the spirits with his word, and healed all that were sick:
*Matthew 8:16*

And Jesus went forth, and saw a great multitude, and was moved with compassion toward them, and he healed their sick.
*Matthew 14:14*

And Jesus went about all Galilee, teaching in their synagogues, and preaching the gospel of the kingdom, and healing all manner of sickness and all manner of disease among the people.
*Matthew 4:23*

Now when the sun was setting, all they that had any sick with divers diseases brought them unto him; and he laid his hands on every one of them, and healed them.
*Luke 4:40*

He sent his word, and healed them, and delivered them from their destructions.
*Psalm 107:20*

Who his own self bare our sins in his own body on the tree, that we, being dead to sins, should live unto righteousness: by whose stripes ye were healed.
*1 Peter 2:24*

Is any among you afflicted? let him pray.
*James 5:13*

Is any sick among you? let him call for the elders of the church; and let them pray over him, anointing him with oil in the name of the Lord:
And the prayer of faith shall save the sick, and the Lord shall raise him up; and if he have committed sins, they shall be forgiven him.
*James 5:14-15*

They shall lay hands on the sick, and they shall recover.
*Mark 16:18*

# Prayer

Enter into his gates with thanksgiving, and into his courts with praise: be thankful unto him, and bless his name.
*Psalm 100:4*

And I say unto you, Ask, and it shall be given you; seek, and ye shall find; knock, and it shall be opened unto you.
*Luke 11:9*

Behold, I am the LORD, the God of all flesh: is there any thing too hard for me?
*Jeremiah 32:27*

And Jesus looking upon them saith, With men it is impossible, but not with God: for with God all things are possible.
*Mark 10:27*

Therefore I say unto you, What things soever ye desire, when ye pray, believe that ye receive them, and ye shall have them.
*Mark 11:24*

Call unto me, and I will answer thee, and show thee great and mighty things, which thou knowest not.
*Jeremiah 33:3*

And whatsoever ye shall ask in my name, that will I do, that the Father may be glorified in the Son.
*John 14:13*

Again I say unto you, That if two of you shall agree on earth as touching any thing that they shall ask, it shall be done for them of my Father which is in heaven.
*Matthew 18:19*

Let us therefore come boldly unto the throne of grace, that we may obtain mercy, and find grace to help in time of need.
*Hebrews 4:16*

O thou that hearest prayer, unto thee shall all flesh come.
*Psalm 65:2*


In the day of my trouble I will call upon thee: for thou wilt answer me.
*Psalm 86:7*


I called upon the LORD in distress: the LORD answered me, and set me in a large place.
*Psalm 118:5*


Blessed be the LORD, because he hath heard the voice of my supplications.
*Psalm 28:6*


Blessed be God, which hath not turned away my prayer, nor his mercy from me.
*Psalm 66:20*


But thou, when thou prayest, enter into thy closet, and when thou hast shut thy door, pray to thy Father which is in secret; and thy Father which seeth in secret shall reward thee openly.
*Matthew 6:6*

But when ye pray, use not vain repetitions, as the heathen do: for they think that they shall be heard for their much speaking.

Be not ye therefore like unto them: for your Father knoweth what things ye have need of, before ye ask him.

*Matthew 6:7-8*


After this manner therefore pray ye:

Our Father which art in heaven, Hallowed be thy name.

Thy kingdom come, Thy will be done in earth, as it is in heaven.

Give us this day our daily bread.

And forgive us our debts, as we forgive our debtors.

And lead us not into temptation, but deliver us from evil:

For thine is the kingdom, and the power, and the glory, for ever. Amen.

*Matthew 6:9-13*


And he spake a parable unto them to this end, that men ought always to pray, and not to faint;

*Luke 18:1*

Be careful for nothing; but in every thing by prayer and supplication with thanksgiving let your requests be made known unto God.
And the peace of God, which passeth all understanding, shall keep your hearts and minds through Christ Jesus.
*Philippians 4:6-7*

Likewise the Spirit also helpeth our infirmities: for we know not what we should pray for as we ought: but the Spirit itself maketh intercession for us with groanings which cannot be uttered.
*Romans 8:26*

If any of you lack wisdom, let him ask of God, that giveth to all men liberally, and upbraideth not; and it shall be given him.
*James 1:5*

Pray without ceasing.
*1 Thessalonians 5:17*

# Provision

I have been young, and now am old; yet have I not seen the righteous forsaken, nor his seed begging bread.
*Psalm 37:25*

For he shall deliver the needy when he crieth; the poor also, and him that hath no helper.
*Psalm 72:12*

For thou hast been a strength to the poor, a strength to the needy in his distress, a refuge from the storm, a shadow from the heat, when the blast of the terrible ones is as a storm against the wall.
*Isaiah 25:4*

When the poor and needy seek water, and there is none, and their tongue faileth for thirst, I the LORD will hear them, I the God of Israel will not forsake them.
*Isaiah 41:17*

He raiseth up the poor out of the dust, and lifteth up the beggar from the dunghill, to set them among princes, and to make them inherit the throne of glory:
*1 Samuel 2:8*

Trust in the LORD, and do good; so shalt thou dwell in the land, and verily thou shalt be fed.
*Psalm 37:3*

Therefore I say unto you, Take no thought for your life, what ye shall eat, or what ye shall drink; nor yet for your body, what ye shall put on.
Is not the life more than meat, and the body than raiment?
Behold the fowls of the air: for they sow not, neither do they reap, nor gather into barns; yet your heavenly Father feedeth them.
Are ye not much better than they?
*Matthew 6:25-26*

Wherefore, if God so clothe the grass of the field, which to day is, and to morrow is cast into the oven, shall he not much more clothe you, O ye of little faith?
*Matthew 6:30*

Bring ye all the tithes into the storehouse, that there may be meat in mine house, and prove me now herewith, saith the LORD of hosts, if I will not open you the windows of heaven, and pour you out a blessing, that there shall not be room enough to receive it.
*Malachi 3:10*

Honour the LORD with thy substance, and with the firstfruits of all thine increase:
So shall thy barns be filled with plenty, and thy presses shall burst out with new wine.
*Proverbs 3:9-10*

Thus saith the LORD, thy Redeemer, the Holy One of Israel; I am the LORD thy God which teacheth thee to profit, which leadeth thee by the way that thou shouldest go.
*Isaiah 48:17*

If ye be willing and obedient, ye shall eat the good of the land:
*Isaiah 1:19*

By humility and the fear of the LORD are riches, and honour, and life.
*Proverbs 22:4*

Cast thy bread upon the waters: for thou shalt find it after many days.
*Ecclesiastes 11:1*


Give, and it shall be given unto you; good measure, pressed down, and shaken together, and running over, shall men give into your bosom. For with the same measure that ye mete withal it shall be measured to you again.
*Luke 6:38*


He that hath pity upon the poor lendeth unto the LORD; and that which he hath given will he pay him again.
*Proverbs 19:17*


He that giveth unto the poor shall not lack: but he that hideth his eyes shall have many a curse.
*Proverbs 28:27*


He that hath a bountiful eye shall be blessed; for he giveth of his bread to the poor.
*Proverbs 22:9*

But my God shall supply all your need according to his riches in glory by Christ Jesus.
*Philippians 4:19*


Thou crownest the year with thy goodness; and thy paths drop fatness.
*Psalm 65:11*


Wealth and riches shall be in his house: and his righteousness endureth for ever.
*Psalm 112:3*


The blessing of the LORD, it maketh rich, and he addeth no sorrow with it.
*Proverbs 10:22*


Better is a dinner of herbs where love is, than a stalled ox and hatred therewith.
*Proverbs 15:17*


Blessed be the Lord, who daily loadeth us with benefits, even the God of our salvation.
*Psalm 68:19*

Let the LORD be magnified, which hath pleasure
in the prosperity of his servant.
*Psalm 35:27*

# Protection

After these things the word of the LORD came unto Abram in a vision, saying, Fear not, Abram: I am thy shield, and thy exceeding great reward.
**Genesis 15:1**

No weapon that is formed against thee shall prosper; and every tongue that shall rise against thee in judgment thou shalt condemn.
This is the heritage of the servants of the LORD, and their righteousness is of me, saith the LORD.
**Isaiah 54:17**

When thou passest through the waters, I will be with thee; and through the rivers, they shall not overflow thee: when thou walkest through the fire, thou shalt not be burned; neither shall the flame kindle upon thee.
**Isaiah 43:2**

The name of the LORD is a strong tower: the righteous runneth into it, and is safe.
*Proverbs 18:10*


I will say of the LORD, He is my refuge and my fortress: my God; in him will I trust.
*Psalm 91:2*


The fear of the LORD tendeth to life: and he that hath it shall abide satisfied; he shall not be visited with evil.
*Proverbs 19:23*


Because thou hast made the LORD, which is my refuge, even the most High, thy habitation;
There shall no evil befall thee, neither shall any plague come nigh thy dwelling.
*Psalm 91:9-10*


For he shall give his angels charge over thee, to keep thee in all thy ways.
*Psalm 91:11*

O GOD the Lord, the strength of my salvation,
thou hast covered my head in the day of battle.
*Psalm 140:7*


The LORD is my rock, and my fortress, and my
deliverer; my God, my strength, in whom I will
trust; my buckler, and the horn of my salvation,
and my high tower.
*Psalm 18:2*


For in the time of trouble he shall hide me in his
pavilion: in the secret of his tabernacle shall he hide
me; he shall set me up upon a rock.
*Psalm 27:5*


The LORD is my light and my salvation; whom
shall I fear?
The LORD is the strength of my life; of whom
shall I be afraid?
*Psalm 27:1*


But whoso hearkeneth unto me shall dwell safely,
and shall be quiet from fear of evil.
*Proverbs 1:33*

If God be for us, who can be against us?
*Romans 8:31*


The LORD shall preserve thee from all evil: he
shall preserve thy soul.
The LORD shall preserve thy going out and thy
coming in from this time forth, and even for
evermore.
*Psalm 121:7-8*


In the fear of the LORD is strong confidence: and
his children shall have a place of refuge.
*Proverbs 14:26*


As the mountains are round about Jerusalem, so the
LORD is round about his people from henceforth
even for ever.
*Psalm 125:2*


Blessed is he that considereth the poor: the LORD
will deliver him in time of trouble.
The LORD will preserve him, and keep him alive;
and he shall be blessed upon the earth: and thou
wilt not deliver him unto the will of his enemies.
*Psalm 41:1-2*

Behold, the eye of the LORD is upon them that
fear him, upon them that hope in his mercy;
To deliver their soul from death, and to keep them
alive in famine.
*Psalm 33:18-19*

The LORD also will be a refuge for the oppressed,
a refuge in times of trouble.
*Psalm 9:9*

The LORD shall preserve thee from all evil: he
shall preserve thy soul.
*Psalm 121:7*

I will both lay me down in peace, and sleep: for
thou, LORD, only makest me dwell in safety.
*Psalm 4:8*

For thou hast been a shelter for me, and a strong
tower from the enemy.
*Psalm 61:3*

He disappointeth the devices of the crafty, so that
their hands cannot perform their enterprise.
*Job 5:12*

The LORD is on my side; I will not fear: what can man do unto me?
*Psalm 118:6*


Nay, in all these things we are more than conquerors through him that loved us.
*Romans 8:37*


Yea, though I walk through the valley of the shadow of death, I will fear no evil: for thou art with me; thy rod and thy staff they comfort me.
*Psalm 23:4*


For I am persuaded, that neither death, nor life, nor angels, nor principalities, nor powers, nor things present, nor things to come,
Nor height, nor depth, nor any other creature, shall be able to separate us from the love of God, which is in Christ Jesus our Lord.
*Romans 8:38-39*

# Deliverance

Shall the prey be taken from the mighty, or the lawful captive delivered?
But thus saith the LORD, Even the captives of the mighty shall be taken away, and the prey of the terrible shall be delivered: for I will contend with him that contendeth with thee, and I will save thy children.
*Isaiah 49:24-25*

Because he hath set his love upon me, therefore will I deliver him: I will set him on high, because he hath known my name.
*Psalm 91:14*

He shall call upon me, and I will answer him: I will be with him in trouble; I will deliver him, and honour him.
*Psalm 91:15*

Surely he shall deliver thee from the snare of the fowler, and from the noisome pestilence.
*Psalm 91:3*

Behold, I give unto you power to tread on serpents and scorpions, and over all the power of the enemy: and nothing shall by any means hurt you.
*Luke 10:19*

For this purpose the Son of God was manifested, that he might destroy the works of the devil.
*1 John 3:8*

And it shall come to pass in that day, that his burden shall be taken away from off thy shoulder, and his yoke from off thy neck, and the yoke shall be destroyed because of the anointing.
*Isaiah 10:27*

Stand fast therefore in the liberty wherewith Christ hath made us free, and be not entangled again with the yoke of bondage.
*Galatians 5:1*

Through God we shall do valiantly: for he it is that shall tread down our enemies.
*Psalm 60:12*


And I will deliver thee out of the hand of the wicked, and I will redeem thee out of the hand of the terrible.
*Jeremiah 15:21*


Though I walk in the midst of trouble, thou wilt revive me: thou shalt stretch forth thine hand against the wrath of mine enemies, and thy right hand shall save me.
*Psalm 138:7*


I will call on the LORD, who is worthy to be praised: so shall I be saved from mine enemies.
*2 Samuel 22:4*


Thou art my hiding place; thou shalt preserve me from trouble; thou shalt compass me about with songs of deliverance.
*Psalm 32:7*

He delivered me from my strong enemy, and from them which hated me: for they were too strong for me.
*Psalm 18:17*


Ye shall not fear them: for the LORD your God he shall fight for you.
*Deuteronomy 3:22*


Behold, they shall surely gather together, but not by me: whosoever shall gather together against thee shall fall for thy sake.
*Isaiah 54:15*


The angel of the LORD encampeth round about them that fear him, and delivereth them.
*Psalm 34:7*


How God anointed Jesus of Nazareth with the Holy Ghost and with power: who went about doing good, and healing all that were oppressed of the devil; for God was with him.
*Acts 10:38*

And these signs shall follow them that believe;
In my name shall they cast out devils; they shall
speak with new tongues;
They shall take up serpents; and if they drink any
deadly thing, it shall not hurt them; they shall lay
hands on the sick, and they shall recover.
*Mark 16:17-18*


And when he was come into the house, his disciples
asked him privately, Why could not we cast him
out?
And he said unto them, This kind can come forth
by nothing, but by prayer and fasting.
*Mark 9:28-29*


Put on the whole armour of God, that ye may be
able to stand against the wiles of the devil.
For we wrestle not against flesh and blood, but
against principalities, against powers, against the
rulers of the darkness of this world, against spiritual
wickedness in high places.
*Ephesians 6:11-12*


Verily I say unto you, Whatsoever ye shall bind on
earth shall be bound in heaven: and whatsoever ye
shall loose on earth shall be loosed in heaven.
*Matthew 8:18*

And at midnight Paul and Silas prayed, and sang praises unto God: and the prisoners heard them. And suddenly there was a great earthquake, so that the foundations of the prison were shaken: and immediately all the doors were opened, and every one's bands were loosed.

*Acts 16:25-26*

Oh that men would praise the LORD for his goodness, and for his wonderful works to the children of men!
For he hath broken the gates of brass, and cut the bars of iron in sunder.

*Psalm 107:15-16*

There hath no temptation taken you but such as is common to man: but God is faithful, who will not suffer you to be tempted above that ye are able; but will with the temptation also make a way to escape, that ye may be able to bear it.

*1 Corinthians 10:13*

# Salvation

For God so loved the world, that he gave his only begotten Son, that whosoever believeth in him should not perish, but have everlasting life.
*John 3:16*

Therefore the Lord himself shall give you a sign; Behold, a virgin shall conceive, and bear a son, and shall call his name Immanuel.
*Isaiah 7:14*

For unto us a child is born, unto us a son is given: and the government shall be upon his shoulder: and his name shall be called Wonderful, Counsellor, The mighty God, The everlasting Father, The Prince of Peace.
*Isaiah 9:6*

Jesus saith unto him, I am the way, the truth, and the life: no man cometh unto the Father, but by me.
*John 14:6*

Neither is there salvation in any other: for there is
none other name under heaven given among men,
whereby we must be saved.
*Acts 4:12*


And Jesus said unto them, I am the bread of life:
he that cometh to me shall never hunger;
and he that believeth on me shall never thirst.
*John 6:35*


I am the door: by me if any man enter in, he shall
be saved, and shall go in and out, and find pasture.
*John 10:9*


Behold, I stand at the door, and knock: if any man
hear my voice, and open the door, I will come in to
him, and will sup with him, and he with me.
*Revelation 3:20*


The thief cometh not, but for to steal, and to kill,
and to destroy: I am come that they might have life,
and that they might have it more abundantly.
*John 10:10*

If my people, which are called by my name, shall humble themselves, and pray, and seek my face, and turn from their wicked ways; then will I hear from heaven, and will forgive their sin, and will heal their land.
*2 Chronicles 7:14*

Come now, and let us reason together, saith the LORD: though your sins be as scarlet, they shall be as white as snow; though they be red like crimson, they shall be as wool.
*Isaiah 1:18*

If we confess our sins, he is faithful and just to forgive us our sins, and to cleanse us from all unrighteousness.
*1 John 1:9*

Wherefore come out from among them, and be ye separate, saith the Lord, and touch not the unclean thing; and I will receive you.
And will be a Father unto you, and ye shall be my sons and daughters, saith the Lord Almighty.
*2 Corinthians 6:17-18*

But seek ye first the kingdom of God, and his righteousness; and all these things shall be added unto you.
*Matthew 6:33*


Through the tender mercy of our God; whereby the dayspring from on high hath visited us,
To give light to them that sit in darkness and in the shadow of death, to guide our feet into the way of peace.
*Luke 1:78-79*


Whosoever shall confess that Jesus is the Son of God, God dwelleth in him, and he in God.
*1 John 4:15*


For I am not ashamed of the gospel of Christ: for it is the power of God unto salvation to every one that believeth;
*Romans 1:16*


And it shall come to pass, that whosoever shall call on the name of the Lord shall be saved.
*Acts 2:21*

With long life will I satisfy him, and shew him
my salvation.
*Psalm 91:16*


Jesus answered and said unto him, Verily, verily, I
say unto thee,
Except a man be born again, he cannot see the
kingdom of God.
*John 3:3*


Believe on the Lord Jesus Christ, and thou shalt be
saved, and thy house.
*Acts 16:31*


He that believeth and is baptized shall be saved; but
he that believeth not shall be damned.
*Mark 16:16*


But we believe that through the grace of the LORD
Jesus Christ we shall be saved, even as they.
*Acts 15:11*

The word is nigh thee, even in thy mouth, and in thy heart: that is, the word of faith, which we preach;

That if thou shalt confess with thy mouth the Lord Jesus, and shalt believe in thine heart that God hath raised him from the dead, thou shalt be saved.
*Romans 10:8-9*


But God commendeth his love toward us, in that, while we were yet sinners, Christ died for us.
*Romans 5:8*


Much more then, being now justified by his blood, we shall be saved from wrath through him.
*Romans 5:9*


And this is the record, that God hath given to us eternal life, and this life is in his Son.
*1 John 5:11*


He that hath the Son hath life; and he that hath not the Son of God hath not life.
*1 John 5:12*

For there is one God, and one mediator between God and men, the man Christ Jesus; Who gave himself a ransom for all, to be testified in due time.
*1 Timothy 2:5-6*

Repent, and be baptized every one of you in the name of Jesus Christ for the remission of sins, and ye shall receive the gift of the Holy Ghost.
*Acts 2:38*

I say unto you, that likewise joy shall be in heaven over one sinner that repenteth, more than over ninety and nine just persons, which need no repentance.
*Luke 15:7*

But now in Christ Jesus ye who sometimes were far off are made nigh by the blood of Christ.
*Ephesians 2:13*

Christ hath redeemed us from the curse of the law, being made a curse for us: for it is written, Cursed is every one that hangeth on a tree:
That the blessing of Abraham might come on the Gentiles through Jesus Christ; that we might receive the promise of the Spirit through faith.
*Galatians 3:13-14*

All that the Father giveth me shall come to me; and him that cometh to me I will in no wise cast out.
*John 6:37*


Fear God, and keep his commandments: for this is the whole duty of man.
*Ecclesiastes 12:13*


And he said unto me, It is done. I am Alpha and Omega, the beginning and the end.
I will give unto him that is athirst of the fountain of the water of life freely.
*Revelation 21:6*


He that overcometh shall inherit all things; and I will be his God, and he shall be my son.
*Revelation 21:7*


Blessed are they that do his commandments, that they may have right to the tree of life, and may enter in through the gates into the city.
*Revelation 22:14*

And there shall be no night there; and they need no candle, neither light of the sun; for the Lord God giveth them light: and they shall reign for ever and ever.
*Revelation 22:5*

And I heard a great voice out of heaven saying, Behold, the tabernacle of God is with men, and he will dwell with them, and they shall be his people, and God himself shall be with them, and be their God.
*Revelation 21:3*

And God shall wipe away all tears from their eyes; and there shall be no more death, neither sorrow, nor crying, neither shall there be any more pain: for the former things are passed away.
*Revelation 21:4*